Poems of My Time
(Life in the San Juan Islands)

Written and Illustrated

By

Hugh R. Roberts, jr.

Binford & Mort Publishing, Portland, Oregon

Cover art by Hugh R. Roberts, jr.

Poems of My Time: Life in the San Juan Islands
Copyright © 2000 by Hugh R. Roberts, jr.

All rights reserved. No part of this book may be reproduced in any form or by any means without permission in writing by the author.

Printed in the United States of America

Library of Congress Catalog Card Number: 00-105768

ISBN 0-8323-0564-9

First Edition

Contents

Foreword vii
Acknowledgements viii
Introduction ix

CHAPTER ONE—MEMORIES

Memories 2
Where Lady Slippers Grow 2
The Good Old Days 3
They Came Here Just Ahead of Me 4
When I was Five 6
Islands in the Sound 8
Dusting 8
Islands Rising from the Sea 10
Do You Ever Think of Me? 11
Portland Fair 12
The Circus Came to Town 12
Soft Shoulders 13
Sarah Ruth of Straight Answers 14
Friday's Bay 15
Feeling Nature 16
In Retrospect 17
The Valley Church 18
The Separator 20

CHAPTER TWO—SOME THINGS TO THINK ABOUT

It's Late 22
Thought for Tonight 22
A Timely Thought 23
I'd Pick More Daisies 24
Answer to "The Daisies" 25
Determination 26
Knowledge 26
Perfection 26

CHAPTER THREE—PATRIOTISM

Remember Me? 28
I Placed the Wreath 30
Fly My Flag 31
I Knew Freedom 32

CHAPTER FOUR—JUST FOR FUN

To Gomez 34
The Smells I Like 35
A Modest Hero 36
Food Stuff 38
Fly or Float 39
Orcas Belle 39
Rosa Mendoza 40
Pictures 41
The Book Report 44
Just a Thought 44

CHAPTER FIVE—LOVE AND WILD ROSES

Cattle Point 46
Blast Those Wild Roses! 47
Has Summer Passed? 47
To a Queen 48
The Sound 49
To Mom 50
The Song of Love 51
I Love a Cow 52
Wild Pink Roses 54
Oh, Precious Little Imp 55
The Rain 56
About Love 56
Another Wild Rose 57
Little Yellow Gold Finch 58

CHAPTER SIX—WINTER TIME

Winter Winds 60
Winter at the Door 63
Snow Flakes 64
Deep Snow 64
The Snowman 64

CHAPTER SEVEN—OF THIS AND THAT

Buy a Piece of Life 66
The *Vashon* 67
Goodbye Old Girl! 67
The Carpenter 68
To Sue 69
A Time to Judge 69
Adrift in Life 70
Momma's Pie 71
Play the Game 71
I Saw Them Mourn 72
"T" Time 73
San Juan Park 73
A Trip to the Mainland 74
Taste-bud Temptation 74
Times Have Changed 75
I Let My Honored Dead Depart 76

Index 77

v

Dedication

To my mother, Lorena Boyce (Roberts) Buchanan
and to my beloved islands.

Foreword

As I read and study the poems and sketches by Hugh Roberts, I wonder what other talents he has kept hidden from view.

Roberts, a very complex man, was deeply influenced by the beauty and forces of nature that strongly regulate life in the San Juan Islands.

This boy from Friday Harbor was molded by these forces: the strong winds that drive and intensify the cold winter snows, the mountains and lush meadows dotted with small farms, islands surrounded by salty seas, have pounded and formed a small boy into a large, vigorous and proud man.

His mind and body responded through his five senses as he reacted in wonder to the dramatic and seasonal changes in the elements of nature.

The islands offer a structured organization that affected his personal life and profession. His poems are of this man's acceptance and adaptation to the overcast sky, the winter snow, the raging sea, wild pink roses, lush green fields, the smell of sage brush, the smell of the Sound and even to the affection for his cow.

Mr. Roberts' profession was structured and orderly—law enforcement. As a police chief he allowed others to live an orderly life directed, not by the force of nature, but one dictated by the will of the people.

Order brings freedom to the spirit of man, leading to happiness as its finest reward.

"No where on earth are you more free than in the islands..." (*Orcas Belle*).

Can one really determine if his poems originate from his sketches, or his sketches from his poems?

Perhaps Volume II, 1969 to 2000, will reveal more.

Robert B. Miller, jr. MS, OD, JD

Acknowledgements

I owe an expression of thanks to Marvin R. Wallace, my "good writing buddy," for the encouragement he has given me during our "adventures" in writing from our days at Marylhurst to now.

I am grateful to Harlene Gallanger for proof reading, grammar checking and other helpful suggestions. I appreciate my children, who have be subject matter of some of the poems and who have warmly encouraged this project.

I am especially grateful to my sweet wife, Jane, for her patience, encouragement, time spent in reading and listening to and for corrections and suggestions; but most of all for being my greatest fan.

Introduction

The San Juan Islands are my home, namely San Juan Island where I grew up, but Orcas Island was also my home for quite a number of years while our children were growing up. I can honestly say my roots are deeply planted in the islands.

My parents, grandparents, great-grandparents and great-great-grandparents were San Juan Islanders. My great-great-grandmother was the first white woman on San Juan and my great-great-grandfather the first sheriff in San Juan county. Their homestead was at Kanaka Bay and granddad courted my grandmother by walking over Sugar Loaf mountain to Mitchell Bay on the opposite side of the island.

My love of poetry came from my mother, who read to us from an old book of English and New England poets on long winter nights while we cuddled up next to her by a warm, crackling wood-fire, the freezing winter winds howling, scraping the rose bushes against the side of the house and at times, shaking the house itself, with the force of the gale.

In the islands of the 1930s—and even into the seventies—it was not infrequent to be without electricity for days on end in the winter. I saw my first television in 1951; it was not very impressive, to say the least.

The islands were pretty secluded. When the Vashon started its run from Anacortes to Friday Harbor, it left Friday Harbor in the morning at six thirty a.m. and returned in the evening, one trip a day.

The mail service was contracted out at various times to the *Chickawana*, the *Osage*, out of Bellingham and the *Water Baby* hauled the mail from Anacortes to the islands.

Medical emergencies were evacuated on the Coast Guard cutter stationed at Friday Harbor. Later the Coast Guard performed the same service with a seaplane. Bruce McKenzie had a seaplane about 1939 or so, but there were no other private airplanes in the islands until after World War II, when the Savage brothers, Bill and Bob, came to San Juan with their pontoon planes and Roy Franklin with his land plane.

Later, Dr. Malcolm Heath served all the islands with his Piper Cherokee, flying in all kinds of weather.

Telephones were of the old wall-mounted hand-crank type clear up into the late fifties or early sixties and were strictly party line. There were always those who "rubbered" in on your phone calls. The more people who listened in the less audio volume one had. I remember mother more than once asking "Mrs. So and So" to get off the line so she could hear.

"I'll call you back and tell you what we talked about, if you'd like." There would be a click on the phone and reception suddenly improved markedly.

Operators were notorious for listening in to phone calls as well. On one occasion there was a house fire that destroyed a local home. A family member placed a long distance call to a hotel in Bellingham to inform the relative of the disaster; the operator, my grandmother, listened in.

"She's gone, cousin!"

"Good! Good! I'll be home in the morning!"

If telepathy thrived, so did bootlegging.

The sheriff had been trying to catch some bootleggers for quite some time. He would call the Coast Guard and alert them to the impending raid.

"Chief, it's on for tonight. The boys are going to bring in a shipment!"

"Right, Sheriff! We'll get underway now!" The cutter would sweep in from the Southwest side, plowing into the bay, cutting off the escape route, while the sheriff came in on land and would scoop them up.

But it was almost uncanny, they were never able to catch the smugglers. That is, until it dawned on them, the operator (not my grandmother) was related to the smugglers. By arranging a coded message they were finally able to coordinate the raid and caught my other relatives in the act.

With happenings like this, we didn't need television.

CHAPTER ONE

"MEMORIES"

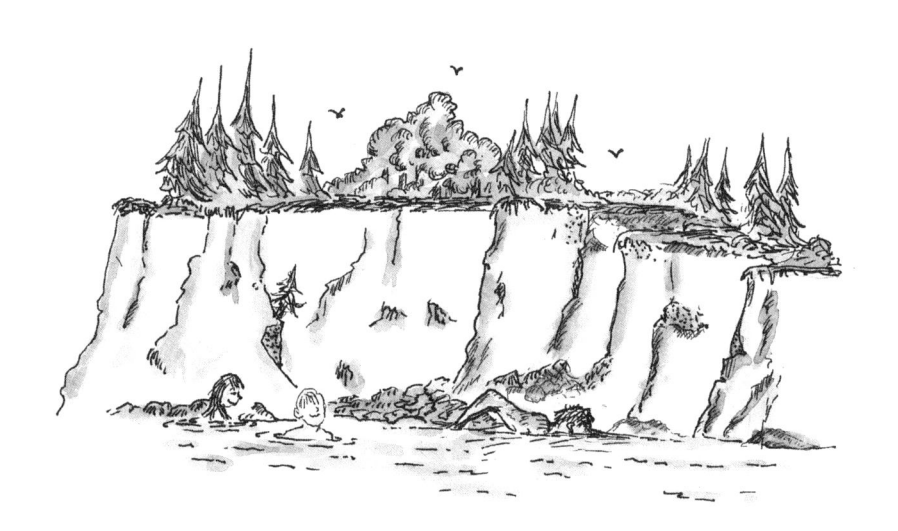

Memories

  School days of long ago,
Rising sun and starry nights;
  Friends and winter snow;
The bay and soft warm lights.
  Hay, fresh cut, upon the ground;
Cows and horses in the stall;
  Lapping water in the Sound;
Fish boats in the Fall.
  Work and play and lots of fun,
With other boys and girls
  Swimming in the island sun,
Watching icy eddy swirls.
  Loving all the years gone by.
Memories sweet of long ago;
  Puffy clouds and deep blue sky
And all of you I know.

Where Lady Slippers Grow

In the woods, in secret spots
The Lady Slippers live;
Among the trees where needles brown,
Rich bedding to them give.
In shady spots kissed by the sun
In Springtime's early hours
Grow these dainty long-stemmed rare
And very pretty flowers.

I read somewhere they are but few
And in the East they grow,
But mother found them growing wild
In places I now know.
These lovely ladies of our isles, where
Mom grew up as well,
Still grow in secret places there,
Where? I will never tell.

The Good Old Days

Oh, for the good old days I say,
When the farmer shocked the new mown hay,
And sent his boy to the field for the cows,
While his wife took mash and slop to the sows.

Oh, for the good old days, I say,
When the neighbor rounded up your stray,
Or, helped you build another barn
And the women manufactured yarn.

Oh, for the days that long are past,
And the time that traveled by so fast,
That left the farmer with an aged frame
And a gnarled leg that's a little game.

Oh, for the days that now are spent,
That left his wife so thin and bent,
With all the aches the bones now feel
And gone is all the youthful zeal.

Oh, for the good old days, I say?
Thank goodness they have gone away!
For now that working days are past,
This old man can rest at last.

They Came Here Just Ahead of Me
And I Ahead of You

The trees stood tall and murmured
    To the breezes gentle kiss;
The sun reflected on the bay—
    On silent wings the sea gulls soared;
The meadows smelled of berries red and black,
    And great-grandma stood in wonder.
See. . . she came here just ahead of me:
    And I ahead of you.

The piling rocked to heavy swells;
    The fish thrashed in the net.
The sky was overcast and cold;
    The wind from the south and west.
The fish trap, stolid and alone,
    Stood on the South-end's graveled beach;
And granddad straightened from his task
    To breathe the salt-spiced air.
See. . . He came here just ahead of me:
    And I ahead of you.

I have seen the sunrise from on these rocky shores;
    I've watched the moon rise silently
Above the blackened sentry trees;
    And listened to the night-hawk thrum
As they flitted in the dark.
    I've watched the freighters, *Indian*, and *Mohawk*
    Ply their trade around the isles.
See . . . they came here just ahead of me:
    And I ahead of you.

Now, when I'm gone, my sons,
        And lady slippers bloom no more
In secret spots I knew so well,
        Who will smell the fir trees scent
And watch the kelp beds rise and fall?
        What room is there for you?
Ah, well;
        Remember what I say:
You came here just ahead of them:
        And I ahead of you.

When I Was Five

When I was five, I loved to walk across the farm
And, holding Daddy's hand,
      We'd find a thousand new designs
As we shared our woodsy land:
When I was five.

When I was five, we lay in grass 'most tall as me
And chewed the stem;
      We laughed and talked together;
Watched the foxes, with Heidi after them:
When I was five.

When I was five, the troubles of the world
Disappeared and I was glad.
      Nothing but the smell of fir and grass and fern;
Then I knew dad;
When I was five.

When I was five, the berries wild and red,
Like a carpet grew at home,
      And Dad would pick them for my mouth;
I would eat them, then the field I'd roam;
When I was five.

When I was five, I had to pick those berries,
Juicy tender berries sweet,
      Wild strawberries, made by God,
For the little folks to eat;
When I was five.

When I was five, my dad would take my hand,
Warm it with his own;
      He'd tell me stories; listen to my questions;
And hold me;
When I was five.

When I was five, the earth was filled with song
And nature's beauty everywhere;
 My eyes would dance with merriment,
It would banish all the care;
When I was five.

When I was five, I knew the joy of being loved,
And having loved I grew;
 When the years had passed,
Life had left its furrows on my brow;
Then I knew I had been loved,
When I was five.

Islands in the Sound

The sound of water lapping on the shore,
        With a winter breeze,
Or, on the coming tide,
        Is cold and green and brings
A shiver in the rain.
        The mountains rising
From the ocean floor
        Become islands riding
On the Puget Sound,
        With magic trees and ferns
And wild lady slipper flowers.

Dusting

Flapping wings and dust abound,
A hen a-squawking on the ground
And Kip and I, eyes big and wide,
Watched the rooster and his bride;
"Dusting," mother told us then,
"It's how the rooster and the hen
Make baby chicks," so mother tells,
"Fluffy birds in fine brown shells."

One day my eleven year old brother and I were watching the chickens as they scratched the ground for worms and insects. Suddenly, right before our startled eyes, the big Rhode Island Red rooster leaped upon the back of a young hen! She squawked. He pecked her hard on the back of her head as he flapped his wings to maintain his balance.

It was clear to us that nasty old rooster was hurting that poor little hen! We raced to the house yelling, "Momma, Momma! The rooster is hurting the hen!"

Mother came out of the house and took one look and smiled.

"Well boys, he really isn't hurting her; he's 'dusting;' That's how they make baby chicks," she explained, "The rooster jumps on her back and flaps his wings and the dust flies and the eggs become fertilized." We knew baby chicks came out of egg shells.

I won't tell you how many years it was before we learned that "dusting" was a myth. Suffice it to say we were both grown men with babies of our own.

Islands Rising From The Sea

Islands rising from the sea;
Rich brown soil and moss and fern,
With alder, cedar and great fir tree,
Peopled by the likes of me.

Logs and flotsam on the tide,
Green seaweed and kelp and cod,
Rocks and reefs beneath they hide.
Mariners view, from boats they ride,

Salmon swimming toward the nets,
Chasing herring and minnows small,
Unaware of traps and sets;
That could settle the fisherman's debts.

Islands rising from the sea,
Scattered in the icy Sound,
Trees and creatures wild and free,
And peopled by the likes of me.

Do You Ever Think of Me?

I don't know why, today, I thought of you;
    I heard the clock ticking on the mantle
In the silent sun-lit room . . .
    (Leaves tell me Fall is here)

I saw your laughing eyes and blushing cheeks,
    Your fair, light hair, gently lifted
With a cool October breeze . . .
    (And first frost arrived last night)

So many memories of you I can recall;
    Sunny afternoons and moonlit winter nights
School bus rides and early morning talks. . .
    (All the pumpkins now are orange)

I still remember just how shy you were,
    And I was very much a rogue I know,
Teasing you until you laughed a pretty laugh. . .
    (My little girl just called to me)

Visits at your house were fun, I liked your mom—
    I liked your daddy too, and Kenny was a boy
Who showed strong promise of a grown up man . . .
    (Her throat, she said, is sore)

I don't know why, today, I thought of you;
    But I am glad I did, for you were very nice,
A special girl, not unlike the one I wed . . .
    (I've aged a bit, have you?)

Although we never see each other now,
    I still remember you, a very special friend,
And sometimes wonder how you are and . . .
    (Do you ever think of me?)

Portland Fair

Why they called it "Portland Fair,"
A hill that overlooked the strait,
I think I'll never know.
Vancouver Island, clear in winter sun,
Twenty miles or so away,
Where great-granddad used to go.
Courtship on his mind,
He'd sail or row across the Sound
To see the girl he wished to wed.
From Portland Fair I'd picture that
And feel the sunshine's warmth,
An old clock ticking above my head.

The Circus Came to Town

Mother was a youngish girl
When the circus came to town;
It didn't stay for very long.
Some wagons might have broken down;
Below the hill of Portland Fair,
On False Bay road at Johnson's farm
I saw one sitting on the curve,
I guess it did no harm,
Along beside the gravel road,
When I was just a little boy;
Old and weathered yellow paint,
Wheel spokes that now were broke.
The *rumor* was some snakes had got away.
"When was the circus here?"
I'd ask my mom at different times.
"When I was just a youngish girl," she'd say.

Soft Shoulders

On the road, toward False Bay,
        There is a sign, so people say,
That warns a driver to beware:
        There are soft shoulders lurking there.

On other roads around the isle,
        There are signs of standard style;
But none that would delineate,
        Or, even tend to indicate,
Which warns a driver to beware:
        There are soft shoulders lurking there.

There is one sign that caught my eye
        (And signs, we know, would never lie),
On the road, toward False Bay,
        Whose message, many people say,
Warns a driver to beware:
        There are soft shoulders lurking there.

Sarah Ruth of Straight Answers

Seated on the floor, in front of the fireplace, working on an electrical switch, I felt a small hand placed firmly, but gently, on my shoulder.

"Fawthur," my six year old angel of the long blonde hair began, "Will you answer a straight question for me?"

"Ahhh, if I can I will," I replied somewhat absently.

"Well, Fawthur, does it make Satan happy when a person uses a bad word?"

"Hmmm; Yes I guess it does."

"Fawthur, does he have a smile on his face?"

She now had my full attention.

"Yes, I'm sure he does," I replied.

Patting my shoulder, she concluded as she walked away, "Thank you for the straight answer!"

Friday's Bay

Sleek vessels gliding through the bay;
    Fog horn not so far away;
A misty blanket hides the shore.
    Emptied Buyers go for more.

Friday's bay as smooth as glass,
    Hissing wake as the fish boats pass.
Other boats at the cannery's side;
    Old *Fort Bragg*, on the flooding tide,

Reliance and *Neried* from a by-gone day;
    Newer boats have passed away.
Diesel fuel and creosote:
    Pungent smells from the fishing boat.

Fish boats riding on the clear green tide
    Spreading giant nets out wide,
Rock salt, fresh new paint and rope
    And fishermen filled with more than hope,

To catch a catch of mighty size
    To pay for parts and new supplies,
And leave a bag of dollar bills
    To buy a cabin in the hills.

Or, to get a house right near the shore
    With a window pane in the big front door;
A fine front window and a great fir tree
    And other boats upon the sea.

Feeling Nature

The fog lays in below the hill,
Beneath the ridge by Lawson's mill;
Along the creek all edged in frost,
The countryside is nearly lost
Where giant maples stand and spread
Their golden blankets overhead.

The fields are rich with yellow wheat,
A treasure at the gleaner's feet.
In the meadow, in the dawn,
Before the feeding deer are gone,
A lark begins to call his roll,
The rabbit sits beside his hole,

Before the bee is from her hive,
And all the world is yet alive,
The sun comes peeking through the mist,
Warming everything he's kissed;
Promising a brighter day
To scent the meadow's ripening hay.

I rise and stretch and inhale deep
And wipe my eyes of last night's sleep,
While giving off a mighty yawn
Precipitated by the dawn.
It's then I come to understand
How much I love this bounteous land.

**Those found on the sidelines of life
will also be found on the sidelines of eternity.**

In Retrospect

In retrospect we oft review
The by-gone days, as old men do;
    And dream of giant ocean ships
Tied up in port at foreign slips.
    Smelling tar and creosote
With seagulls perched on every float.

Or, dream we do of smaller craft:
Of sleek trim lines from fore and aft;
    Their shiny painted hulls a-bob,
That did the night-time fishing job.
    Gill netters these, that still remind
(On roughened seas) of frail mankind,
    Who ply their wares from in the sea,
In vessels made from the cedar tree;
    Whose ribs are oak, the fir for mast;

    All made to stand the rudest blast.
But, we recall the smallest part,
    As if it isn't in our heart,
To remember nights of fruitless pain,
    Icy winds that numbed the brain;
Nor bloodied hands from pulling net—
    How could anyone forget?

But, we do, in retrospect,
    Stories carefully select,
That thrills the novice to the core
    Whose feet press firmly on the shore.

The Valley Church

Out on the hill, within the wall
Of graying, granite mossy stone,
Reside the men and women all,
In wormy wood, their dust and bone.

        They rest beneath a quilt of earth,
        Laid to sleep below the sod,
        Grown and died long after birth
        And now they've gone back to their God.

They built the church near where they're laid
A hundred years or more ago,
With tools crude and now decayed,
They split roof shakes with shiny froe.

        The same froe rusted in the post
        (The hickory handle long since gone
        To join the froe-man's ancient ghost)
        Remains with cedar logs he's sawn,

That made the beams of floor and joist,
And giant rafters overhead
By arm and shive-block they did hoist
Before they laid themselves to bed.

        The women came there at the noon
        Baskets heaped with home-made fare,
        To feed them with their pewter spoon
        And bless the food with greatest care.

Then, when the day had waned and past,
They gauged their joy by what they'd wrought;
The frame was done and made to last;
In their tiredness they caught

A glimpse of Heaven's holy light
And knew the edifice they'd made
Had been with more than mortal might.
They knelt in humbleness and prayed.

    Now a century has gone,
    With all that bended to the task;
    Now sleeping in the foggy dawn
    Beneath a granite headstone mask.

Still, we forget their toils and woe,
That made the world in which we live
A better place for us to grow,
And fail our thankful prayers to give.

The Separator

Born too late I was,
    Perhaps by fifty years—
Or more—It's hard to say;
    Nor shall I ever know.
Though not so late
    I can't recall a lot
About those by-gone days of yore;
    That might surprise you some.
I found a paper tucked
    Inside a separator once:
"1904" it said,
    Upon its iron sides;
'13 was on the paper
    Stuffed inside all these many years:
"Cabbage 2 cents a pound!"
    It struck me nearly dumb.
Before my time,
    But just the same I knew,
For many times I cranked it—
    Not *that* one, though alike;
No stranger is the farm,
    Nor lantern lighted cows.
I've bathed beneath a pitcher pump,
    Naked as a jay in an old wash tub.
I've hiked out in the snow,
    I have before,
To early morning chores at dawn,
    To slop the hogs
With home grown grain we've ground.
    I know the feel of life;
I know a bit of living long ago
    I've had history's shoulder rub.

CHAPTER TWO

"SOME THINGS TO THINK ABOUT"

It's Late

    One morning I awoke and glanced at the clock:
Five a.m.
    "It's early," I said.
    Some one else said, "It's late." I rolled over
Ignoring that.
    "I said, 'It's late.' " I pretended I didn't hear.
Then it hit me: No one else should be in the room; I sat up.
    "Who are you?" I asked. A tall stranger stood at
My bedside; he had a determined look.
    "How did you get in here?"
    "I've brought you a message," he replied without
Answering my question, "You have squandered, wasted and
Frittered away forty years of your life; it's late, but you
Still have time—however, you had better get a move on."
    I thought on that for a moment, then closed
My eyes and leaned back against the pillow. When I opened
Them he was gone.
    I wonder who he was? Well, anyway, time marches on.

Thought for Tonight

Between the tide, the currents pull,
The lunar plays, the moon is full.
The sea, green dark, is capped in white;
Celestial bodies hurl in flight.
Slimy denizens swimming past,
Wild comets burn their last.
A mountain range beneath the sea?
The universe still beckons me.
The ocean swallows up her dead;
The sky is not without its dread.
The floods once covered all on earth,
But man's celestial at his birth.

A Timely Thought

   Time has fled before I knew;
All the yesterdays that were
   Are gone.
In the reddened east the clouds;
   Today is but a passing hour,
Lost forever in the fading dawn.
   For but a span the brilliant day
Has gilded all that it has touched
   And leaves the cold engulfing night
To take its charge through
   Marching hours.
Our life is all too short a fight;
   And we cannot a second spare.
All the passing cavalcade
   Are shadows on the walls of time.
Disappearing in the mists
   Of swift eternity that glides.
Seek to be the kind of one
   Who loves, and can forgive a wrong;
But still be strong enough to stand
   The raging tempest in the night.
That when the dawn breaks
   Warm and clear
We stand in gratitude.

I'd Pick More Daisies

If I had my life to live over, I'd pick more daisies. I'd try to make more mistakes next time. I would be sillier than I had been this trip. I would limber up. I know very few things I would take seriously. I would take more trips, travel lighter. I would be crazier. I would be less hygienic. I would take more chances. I would climb more mountains, swim more rivers, and watch more sunsets. I would eat more ice cream and less beans. I would have more actual troubles and fewer imaginary ones.

You see, I am one of those people who live practically and sensible and sanely, hour after hour, day after day... Oh, I have had my mad moments and if I had it to do over again, I'd have more of them. In fact, I'd try to have nothing else. Just moments, one after another, instead of living so many minutes ahead. I have been one of those people who never go any where without a road map, a thermometer, a hot water bottle, a gargle and a raincoat.

If I had my life to live over, I would start barefooted earlier in the spring, and stay that way later in the fall. I'd play hooky more. I would do more water and sun-fun things. I'd turn more somersaults and roll in the grass and go barefoot all over.

If I had my life to live over, I'd spend more time at fun places. I'd try to be more in touch with God and those I love. I'd pray aloud more and not care what people think or expect of me. I'd give more of me and take more of you. I'd just be more and more . . .

Yes, I'd pick more daisies . . . next time.
—Author Unknown—

While attending College I took a poetry class; The class was assigned to respond to the above.

Answer "To the Daisies"

I really have no need to live life over and my regrets would be in vain. Besides, I've done it all. All the things a boy—and a man—want to do.

I've shocked the new mown hay. Driven horse teams so large I couldn't see over them, and the clear blue skies, I've seen with pure white clouds, like fishing boats at anchor.

I have seen pure white falling snow, fence top deep, and the icicles frozen on the dock from the salty spray. I've ridden on the storm. . . in the storm. . . and beneath the stormy sea, with great green walls of water burying and resurrecting me.

I've sailed in little ships and great ships; flown above the clouds, in the clouds and traveled to far off lands and stood barefoot in the sand and snow.

My hands have grasped the iron rod and held a tiny baby girl and boy. My eyes have seen man die in violence and new life ushered in with pains of labor: a taking and a giving.

I've ridden in the mountains on a sure-footed horse, bathed in an icy stream near the mining ghost of LaPlatt and caught trout with bare, frozen hands.

Once, on a high winding trail, I dove, on a dare, into a freezing shallow mountain stream from a rustic log bridge and laughed with twinkling eyes from the sheer love of life.

Danger has been my companion in many forms. We have drunk together the intoxicating liquor made from wild adrenaline, and I have fought for life—but never taken life, for it's too dear.

Last night my children asked about the *old days*, "what were they like?" Am I so old **my** youth is now the **olden days**?

                    I am.

Determination

Determination, I am told,
Is not possessed by bags of gold;
Nor does it come by right of birth
To every person upon this earth,
But must be purchased by a man
Through humble words: "I know I can!"

Knowledge

Knowledge is another case,
Possessed by every different race.
Though used in many different ways
And learned through endless passing days,
It must be purchased by a man,
Through humble words: "I know I can!"

Perfection

Perfection is the final state
For both the husband and his mate;
Obtained through diligence in life
By overcoming grief and strife;
It must be purchased by a man
Through humbly proving: "I know I can!"

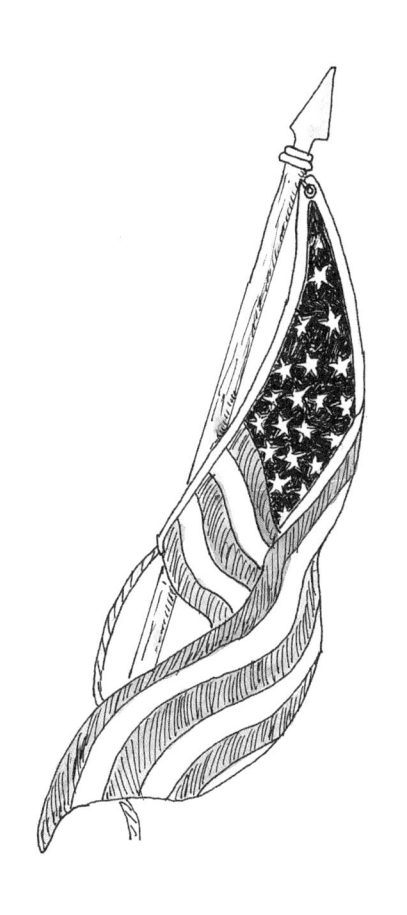

CHAPTER THREE

"PATRIOTISM"

Remember Me?

Remember me? I came here from
Across the sea—
There came a group of friends
With me;
We spent a frozen winter, cold
And wet—a nasty spell.
We really didn't do so well;
But we stayed and worked
And fought,
We earned everything we got.

Remember me? I fought at Concord;
Brave men died.
What if no one even tried?
Think our flag would be the same—
Or, slave-like walk around in shame?
But, we dared, we worked and fought;
We earned everything we got.

Remember me? I fought with Lincoln's boys;
There was lots of death and noise.
We died for what we thought was right;
We bled and gave from dawn 'til night.
But we stayed, we worked and fought;
We earned everything we got.

Remember me? I went to war across the sea;
I marched in France and Germany;
We slogged through mud and made our stand;
We marched across a dying land.
But, we dared, we worked and fought;
We earned everything we got.

Remember me? I died on Iwo's * bloody sands;
I fought with torn and bloodied hands
And gave my life that you might live:
What more can anybody give?
But, we dared, we worked and fought;
We earned everything we got.

Remember me? I'm the one who through the years
Has died and given sweat and tears,
To see *you* had a country free;
Now will you give your life for *me*?
You see, we dared, we worked and fought,
We earned everything *you* got!

* Iwo Jima, an island in the South Pacific, where a terrible battle was fought in World War II.

I Placed the Wreath

I placed the wreath that special day,
As little children and old folks too,
Stood and watched and heard the bugle play.
Some shed tears, as some will do.
I knew back then, although a boy,
That sometimes duty takes away.
For wars can and will destroy.
I placed the wreath that special day.

Fly My Flag

Fly my flag: Proudly—but in humility.
Raise it up above the rest
With greatest dignity.
See its red—the white—the blue?
It's mine!
God made it so—and it's yours too:
If you will take the time.
Fly my flag with bosom filled to overflow;
Put it high above the town
So it will show!
Let a tear fall down your cheek
Unabashed sincerity.
Tell every one how men have died
Of great ability,
That a nation's flag might wave on high:
For you and me.
Don't forget the price others paid
Again may be.
If the price is asked, must we
Lay our bodies by?
Is the cost too much, if we must pass and die?
Fly my flag! The red, the white, the blue!
And if I lose my life, drape me with that flag,
For I die for you.

I Knew Freedom

I knew freedom,
When our laws were less demanding;
I knew freedom,
When men were bravely standing.

Before this crazy fantasy,
Our nation owes our living;
Before this crazy fantasy,
We must be more forgiving.

I knew freedom,
When people earned the right.
I knew freedom,
And basked in freedom's light.

There was a time,
When we could speak of God;
There was a time,
When our flag we could applaud.

I knew freedom,
In those days I had free speech;
I knew freedom,
But now, it's nearly out of reach.

CHAPTER FOUR

"JUST FOR FUN"

To Gomez

Here lies young Gomez, a very strange lad,
Who did nothing good—but he did nothing bad.
By no means a weakling, he had little strength,
And lived not a short life, nor one of much length.

His mind was not great and he had little skill,
He was certainly no moron and worked with a will.
Wealth was a stranger, though he wanted for naught;
He took what he wanted and bought what he got.

He smiled not at all, nor wore he a frown,
When one lip went up, the other went down.
He ended his life in a typical state:
He tried to do nothing 'til it was too late.

The Smells I Like

I like the smell of berry pie;
It brings a twinkle to my eye.
I like the smell of cinnamon toast,
To me it's just about the most.
I like rhubarb, nice and hot,
Bubbling in the cooking pot.
I like the smell of baking beans,
I'll eat them 'til I bust my seams.
I like the smell of baking bread,
Its incense wafts about my head.
I like the roast, so sweet and rare,
It makes a lovely bill of fare.
I like the smell of sage brush too,
When from the range it's fresh and new.
I even like to smell the cow,
In fact, I think I smell her now!
I like the salty ocean air,
Whipping at my short cropped hair.
I like the smell of new mown hay,
The smell that permeates the day.
I like the smell of mountain pine,
That really makes me mighty fine!
I like the lilacs on the tree,
It's such a smell that gets to me.
I like to smell so many things.
Scents that to my memory brings:
I like the smell of peaches sweet,
A lovely treat that can't be beat.
I like the smell of perfumed hair,
From a damsel choice and fair.
In short, I like the smell of things;
I like the smells that summer brings.
So keep in mind what I have said
And slice a slice of home made bread.

A Modest Hero

Around the world I travel,
Every day or so;
I sail in all the finest ships
Everywhere I go.
My men make up the bravest crew
That's found most anywhere;
Two-hundred strong they quick appear
To all the dangers share.

At times when we're surrounded,
By gunboats all around,
My steely voice gives out commands
Through the cannon's thunder sound.

And, standing on the burning bridge,
Not fearing anything,
I spur my crew to harder fight,
Above the battles ring.

Now, when the battles over
And we've beaten nearly all,
I allow them to surrender,
With proper protocol.

Then off I go with orders
To far off foreign lands,
Where I am always greeted
By hordes on every hand.

In France, I'm always recognized
As best of all the lot;
While in dear old England
With the queen I have a "spot."

The rulers of the eastern lands
Offer gold and myrrh,
To win me to their side, you see,
They wish to make quite sure.

But, I am very modest—
As well as brave and strong;
So I make sure they understand,
I fight against *all* wrong.

Then when my travels end up,
At dock side, tied I float:
You see, I am the skipper on
The San Juan Island ferry boat!

Food Stuff

My favorite food, tapioca,
Like whipped Jell-O is a treat;
Bread pudding, I'm a-thinkin'
Goes well with prime rib meat.

Rice pudding, rich with raisins,
Tops off a grand big spread
Of gravy and mashed potatoes
Accompanied by home made bread.

Add butter fresh from the churn,
Then you'll see me in great delight,
Consuming all that's before me,
Through the rest of the day and night.

Yes, feed to me in bowls and dishes,
All the wonderful food you can make
And the pounds I add on won't matter
It's only the scales I'll break!

Fly or Float

Man and sea gull both may float,
One in the air, one in a boat;
Man can also soar in the air,
The sea gull doesn't really care.

Orcas Belle

You proudly fly from after mast
    The flag that stands for liberty;
Bobbing on the tide at Orcas landing,
    Free to go and come
Beneath the sun, or canopy of stars.
    Designed by freedom seeking men,
For spirits of the ocean wide:
    The boundless sea.
Swaying gently to and fro,
    The creaking of your ribs and planks
Belie your sturdy spars,
    Canvas wrapped and tied,
Your hatches battened;
    Wheel and rudder firmly strapped in place.
No where on earth
    Are you more free than in the islands,
Where you sail at will.
    In the windy loft,
Where no man ventures long,
    The hand of God reaches out,
While smiling kindly down,
    And blesses you, oh *Orcas Belle*,
With the freedom of the Sound.

Rosa Mendoza

From the tips of her toes-uh,
Miss Rosa Mendoza
Is certainly a strange sorta kit*;
She's not very tall,
A veritable ball,
Of tamales and tacos—
That's it!
In her bright Spanish clothes-uh,
Miss Rosa Mendoza,
Requires more than a glance:
Her hair is most black,
A delectable snack,
Of chorizo and huevos,
Per-chance?

But if you compose-uh,
For Miss Rosa Mendoza,
A poem of considerable mien,
Be sure that it's right,
For in the dark of the night,
She may cause you
Incredible pain!

* A young fox; or, a cute girl (in the modern vernacular)

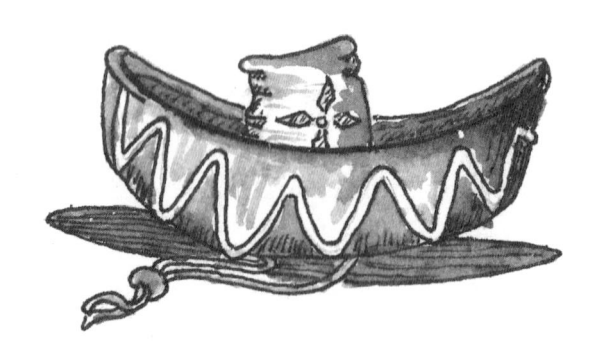

Pictures

I love to draw pictures
Of rabbits and spies,
Of neat little packets
And fast dragon flies.

I draw of such things
As kittens and spooks;
I quite like to draw
Real weird looking kooks!

In meetings I draw
With a vim and a wit
Causing some folks to
Laugh and others to spit.

I love to draw pictures
Of boats sailing the sea,
Or tied at a piling
Which once was a tree.

I sketch little lines
On paper that's white,
I sketch in the day,
Or, I sketch in the night

Making circles and shapes
Which are little or big,
looking something like raisins,
Or tree trunks, or twigs.

I doodle on paper
That's yellow and lined
With pictures apart,
Or all intertwined.

There's pictures of guns
There's one legged lads;
there's drawings of bad guys
And 'Sir Gallahads.'

I make pictures that enter
My mind in a flash,
Dividing the good stuff
From the councilman's trash,

Who sit on the council
and can't draw a line,
But keep sneaking a peek
Of what I've done with mine.

Sometimes they explode,
Like a bomb in a well,
Stones scattered all over,
With a story to tell.
Sometimes I draw nuts
Attached to big bolts
Which break open the thoughts
Of the blithering dolts,

Who chatter and yawn
While they make a decision
As, where the money has gone,
Using oblique tunnel vision.

Or, they pass a new law
That's supposed to do good,
But rather creates
Not that which it should.

Instead of fine lines
On my paper or page,

My thought process prompts me
To wax somewhat sage,

And I draw a fair scene
Of a mountain and plain,
Adding scrubby old trees
And an old logging chain.

I guess this all means,
When taken in thought:
The pictures I draw
Are the pictures I've got.

The Book Report

Within my span of life so short,
    When compared to Adam's time,
I've written quite a book report—
    No commentary at this date.
Suffice to say the pages bulge
    With ventures I have journeyed on
And happenings I won't divulge.

Just a Thought

    Sometimes in the dark of night
I waken with a sudden start;
    Alert to what?
Yesterday I thought of this, alone
    Beside an old brick wall,
I still know not;
    Pussy willows, grand and new,
Rubbed against the brick,
    The crumbling brick,
And I forgot about the dark of night,
    With sudden starts from restless sleep:
The old clock's steady tick;
    Instead I breathed the heady smell
Of mint from fields around the town
    Which told me: Spring is here.

CHAPTER FIVE

"LOVE AND WILD ROSES"

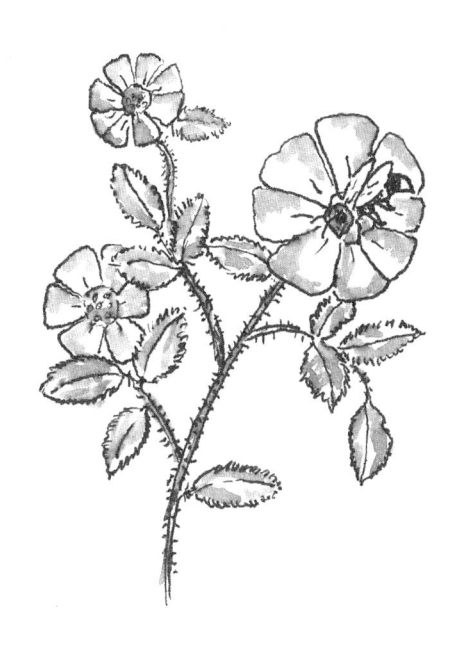

Cattle Point

    Stretching to the South, in rounded hills of sand
And gravel,
    Beneath an azure sky where many people travel,
Covered with sun faded grass and wind swept cape,
    The radio station,* now long gone, remains a
Weathered shape.
    Hills capped by gnarled Douglas giants strong;
A calm and silver sea lies fog-blanketed, but not for long.
    Sea gulls scrap for morsels: Tidbits from the sea,
While herring minnows scatter, for better cover, hastily.
    The surf coldly pounds on the shifting gravel
Beach;
    Timbers flung by greater waves lie stranded
Out of reach.
    Hunched on rocky perches, the lordly eagle
Seeks for prey,
    Keeping watch for silver salmon flashing
In the bay.
    The old South-end, and Salmon Banks, the warm
Lagoon as well,
    Reminds me of my childhood days and stories
I could tell.

    *There was a US Navy Radio station at the South-end, where my dad was stationed in the late 1920s. All that is left now are the concrete walls.

Blast Those Wild Roses!

  Blast those wild roses, with their tiny little leaf,
That cover up so neatly their stalk of spiny teeth;
  Blast them, for it's Springtime and another Winter's gone;
   It simply goes to prove to me that time keeps Marching on.
    Yes, blast the fragile petals of the softest pale Pink,
     Which makes me very much aware of honey Bees, I think.
      Blast them for their pollen and the nectar that They hide;
       For those working little rascals, who honey will Provide.
        Oh, blast them for their tantalizing scent that Tickles at my nose;
         For blasted grateful am I, for the tender wild Rose!

Has Summer passed?

A month ago? No, more, I think.
What? It's November now you say!
Yes, I see the leaves are falling to the ground;
Splendid reds, yellows, and golden brown.
  I guess though Fall is late this year,
  It's clear the summer time has gone.

To a Queen

I won her many years ago,
The time of year when monsoons came.
In a far off oriental land
We hunted hato* in the Fall.

Like Samurai, in war-like dress,
I fought for her and took her hand
By right of victors' royal prize,
And took her to my home.

Across the sea—across the land,
Far from her family still unknown
We wed in sweet solemnity,
Two new and unknown quantities.

Then, time slipped by and babies came;
Each one as welcome as the first
And yet, not free from any rift,
The family circle strained and grew.

Trials in abundance sprang,
They left their mark on aging youth,
Until no more the bride a maid,
Nor groom the carefree, reckless youth.

Until tonight, the setting sun
Came just in time to catch her there,
Standing on the porch alone,
And made her but a girl again.

I spoke, reluctant to intrude,
Unsure, as when a courting youth
I sought to win her heart from her,
Afraid to break the magic spell.

Still, I did, and raised the sun;
From in the west the gold ray touched
And made a girl: No longer wife alone,
But queen of all my realm.

With awe I stood and worshipped her;
In love again, but only more,
And saw us stand in marble halls
Throughout eternity.

*Hato are wild pigeon in Japan

The Sound

Who can hear the Sound?
        Or see and smell the Sound;
Who can know the Sound?
        Or be within and on the Sound;
Who can ride upon the Sound?
        Or be within the icy Sound;
Who can love the Sound?
        Or see the crescent moon above the Sound;

Who, adrift within the fog,
        Upon the Sound, can see a drifting log?
I can. I do!
        Why, it's floating in the Puget Sound,
Riding on the emerald tide
        Where my life's old memories abound.

To Mom

"Hi, Mom!" A greeting that you may recall
From the days when we were small.
When we'd come running in the door
With spirited thoughts that seemed to soar.

"Hi, Mom! We're hungry! What'd you make?"
Or, "How about some chocolate cake?"
Always there, with something good,
To guide her children as she should.

"Hi, Mom! Guess what happened to me today!"
And she would listen in a certain way;
So we knew she always understood
And helped us anyway she could.

"Hi, Mom! Would you read to us awhile?"
She was always with a ready smile,
She gathered us around her chair,
Her soft sweet voice still echoes there.

"Hi, Mom!" Again we say these words to you,
Because of all the things you knew;
For all the good, the loving care
And for the golden thoughts we share.

(Mom's birthday was May 17th and I wrote this poem
for my mother, Lorena Ida Boyce [Roberts] Buchanan.)

The Song of Love

I knew a man, in the season of the year
When the leaves were green
   And the grass was long and lush.

In his heart was a song, you know the one;
You hear it in the gurgling of a brook—
   The warbling of a thrush.

He found it in a wild flower.
He found it in a soft-eyed doe and fawn:
   He heard the night hawk thrum it overhead.

From whence it comes, only heaven knows,
Still, it's in ones heart, deep within;
   Sometimes in a poem you may have read.

The song of love transcends this mortal state;
It liberates the sad and lonely heart;
   It frees the weary longing for the grave.

Its secret passes in a glance between two
Lovers, lost in a world of their own;
   It rides upon a mighty ocean wave.

I knew a man in the season of the year
When breezes cool came from off the sea
   Whispering softly from above.

The song that sang within his heart and soul
That kept him young and full of life,
   Was the song of love.

I Love a Cow

        Why would I. . . could I. . . ever think
A thing like that?
        A bony beast, who ruminates, in fields
Lush and green?
        Would it not make much more sense
To say, "I love a cat?" Perhaps a dog?
        Or, does it not, I would opine,
Sound strange? So it may seem.
        A *cow*? My stars!
I can't believe I'd say, "I love a cow!"
        After all, what's there to love?
She smells of hay and barn.
        But to defend my words so strange,
I'll spell it out right now,
        Without a bit of reddened cheek,
Nor will I spin a yarn.
        Let me just explain without delay,
My affection for a cow:
        I love the way she ambles when she walks
From the field to the barn;
        I love the chewing of her cud
And the fresh hay from the mow,
        Where it is stored for winter time;
Which feeds the worthy beast,
        That gives sweet cream and warm fresh milk
Until the bucket overflows—
        "Sooo, boss. . . Sooo, girl,
I calm her at the evening feast;
        I press my face into her flank
And feel her warmth against the snow,
        I listen to her chew the hay and crunch the grain
Within her jaw.
        And feel the comfort of the time I spend with her.
        I think deep thoughts. . . or ordinary thoughts,

That make a lazy circle in my brain
        Then slip off into the night,
Replaced by new or better thoughts.
        Yes, I love a cow.
For all the reasons that I gave
        And many more I can't explain.

Wild Pink Roses

I walk along the path and see
      Your lacy leaves that beckon me;
Your petals pink, so wild and free,
      The perfume that destroys me:
Wild pink roses.
I gasp to catch another smell
      Of scents so sweet I have to tell
Everyone I see how swell
      To stand beside and dwell upon:
Wild pink roses.
I rush into your knitted thatch
      In hopes that I can snatch
From amidst your greenery patch
      Which I know I cannot catch:
Wild pink roses.
Then all to soon, I've come to fear,
      You vanish for another year
While I shed a silent tear;
      The petals fall and I am near to:
      Wild pink roses.

Oh Precious Little Imp

Oh precious little imp! I know you're six!
I know you're six and still, I look at you
And see my little girl, a baby not so long ago;
Defenseless, pure and sweet and undefiled by age.
Undefiled by wasted time and thoughts—or man.
We walked together down the school's hall.

Your hand so warm and soft in mine:
I almost cried.
When you waved goodbye to me, my heart dissolved.
Dissolved into a giant, lump of putty in your hands.
Oh, precious little imp! The king of fools I am!
Had I but realized how strong your bonds would be,

I might have fought your charms awhile ago!
But, like a little thief, you crept into my heart,
And stole, without a "by your leave" from me!
Oh, precious little imp! How glad I am for you!
For should I leave this earth today I'd know
That from above you came to us in love
And fed your mom and me with laughs and smiles:

A menu far superior to any mortal's tasty meal.
While other times and moments will be yours and mine,
The one today is now a memory, warm and sweet;
One to cherish and remember with the frost:
With the frost that touches every mortal's thatch

(Provided he has been allowed to stay that long).
Oh, precious little imp! From God a spirit free!
Who like a tiny gentle princess, rules within our home:
A gift of love to me!

The Rain

I see the rain.
It falls so fast and hard
It rebounds back again.

I hear the rain.
Beating on the roof so loud
It's like a drum's refrain.

I smell the rain.
And it's so sweet and fresh
All things are clear and clean again.

I see. . . and hear. . . and smell the rain.
And can hardly wait until the sun is high
Enough to dry out all that rain.

About Love

I love the wind,
I love the rain;
I love the whistle of a train.

I love the snow,
I love the sleet;
I love the sound of tiny feet.

I love the sky
That's clear and blue,
But, most of all . . . I just love you!

Another Wild Rose

How I love the wild rose,
In pink and yellow splendor;
I wait and watch their summer entry,
Soft and quiet they unfold.
They sneak into my rolling hills
Green with grasses long and lush.

They come when wild canaries
Wing across the meadow's rolling grasses,
Grasses rolling like a restless sea.
Gold Finches clinging to the fences,
Old and rusty fences,
Sagging with the weight of many years gone by.

It's then I think of mom.
My own dear mom; But then,
I think of her so many other times:
In wild rose time most of all;
The time I miss her here
When a subterranean tear closes with
The surface of my face.

It's when I smell the sweetness of the rose;
The incense in the heavy summer air,
Pulling at my heart, telling me for her:
"Remember me, my son," they seem to say;
"And some fine summer day, you'll see,
The home to which I've flown."

Little Yellow Gold Finch

Little yellow gold finch, with black upon your wing,
Oh, how I like to hear you sing!
I watch the sun-warmed meadows as you pass,
Or, see you swaying on a stem of grass.

Sea gulls play their hunting games for food
Harassed by crows into a fitful mood;
The white topped eagle sits his lofty perch
(Like a sanctimonious preacher in his church)

Head cocked with superiority and disdain,
Displaying to the world his presidential mien
For does a finch, or tern, or gull upon a crest,
Represent a mighty nation blest?

Of course they don't! That mighty bird of prey
Is meant the strength of that great nation to display.
Might not you, our little yellow bird, stand before the world
Upon some standard white and pure unfurled?

Oh, little golden finch you bring the light today,
But, sadly when the summer ends, you go away;
Elusive as a shaft of light you fly,
As if to say: "Catch me! Go ahead and try!

CHAPTER SIX

"WINTER TIME"

Winter Winds

The winter winds blow cold
      And leave their icy traces all about;
No leaves are left upon the trees;
      Long since they've fallen to the ground.
Long since the spring time flowers died
      And Autumn touched with brilliant hue:

It too has disappeared,
      Given way to frosted morning dew
Upon the grass.
      The leaden skies bring silent snow to cap
The fence tops with its pure white flakes:
      To paint a picture clean and pure.

Across the mead, beside the brook
      The icy wind whips brittle wires
And leaves the farm no lights;
      The cattle seek the shelter-barn to
Warm their bony frames and scatter hay—
      And waste—and mud beneath their feet.

The shifting drifts against the house
      Or gates move on,
Yet, still the wind tears at the door and beats
      Upon the window pane.
Coal oil flickers in the lamp, the hearth
      Sends out its glow;

And deep beneath the heavy quilts
      Snuggle little tousled heads
Hiding from the numbing winter wind;
      Protected from its mighty blast
Which rattles glass and window frame.

And slams against the house.
Pictures form in frosty patterns on the pane
    Sending out a chill to all within its
Reach, or who may dare to come too near;
    Even with the shades pulled down
And drapery closed tight against the cold
    And bitter winter night.

Drowsing by the great old stove, the farmer sits,
    Drawing warmth into his frame
After doing battle in the bitter wind and snow;
    Tomorrow is another day
Against the howling angry storm which freezes
    Hands and trees and water pipes.

The North wind clutches at the weathered house
    Of forty gales before;
Creaks and groans of sturdy boards and bats
    Withstand the howling fury of its blast.
Night time passes and dawns another day,
    Beneath another graying sky.

New snow, a blanket, fresh and clean,
    Creates another feather bed;
The posts most near have disappeared,
    The alders bend beneath the weight:
The burden of the snow too much,
    Has broken off a frozen tree.

Over the blackness of the creek
    Snow has built a bridge
On which no man dare plant his feet,
    Or any creature walk,
For fear of its demise,
    Caused by violating natures code.

The roads, hard packed with fresh plowed snow,
        Lay blue against the leaden sky,
Attacked by sleigh and sled
        And happy voices far into the night;
Until the winter winds again have chased these
        Urchins with another freezing blast
Indoors for warmth, against the cold outdoors
        To wait another day to dawn
And winter time to pass.

Winter at The Door

Red, ripe Russets, crispy Kings,
Hanging on their bowing branches cling;
And on the mossy carpet,
They lay scattered all about;
Delicious odor, pungent smell,
In early morn—and dusk—the graceful
Deer they bring.

Red berries of the wild rose and rusting leaves
Of willow, alder, oak and all the rest,
Flutter to the ground, a quilted carpet make.
Quick small birds, darting to and fro,
Usher in the lateness of the Fall.
The Summer season dies to bring another
Season, which also soon must die.

Overhead, in grand formation, the steady geese
Seek a warmer clime;
In loud and raucous voice the duck,
Now fewer than before,
On rapid wing, as other ducks have done,
Flee from the Winter time.

The country side, all about beset by mist
And Winter's foggy vapor,
Lies sleeping still,
As if the Lord has said:
"Hush now and when the Winter's done
Awake refreshed, renewed."

Snowflakes

The snow is blowing in the air,
And lights upon my nose and hair;
Little flakes of purest white,
Fall by day or dark of night
They fall and fly, or swirl away
And no one knows how long they'll stay.

Deep Snow

Snow packed clear up to my knees,
On every plant and on the trees;

          The deepest snow you've ever seen!
          It looks so very white and clean,

But daddy says it isn't much
(Even though it's fun to touch),

          Because it only tops his shoes,
          Isn't that some funny news?

The Snowman

White and fat—
    Well how 'bout that?
        Black coal eyes
And mammoth size!
    Big carrot nose;
        He's darn near froze.
Big Spring rain:
    He's down the drain.

CHAPTER SEVEN

"OF THIS AND THAT"

Buy a Piece of Life

Buy a piece of life for me
And let me live it well;
Let me use it as I wish,
Then have the angels tell.

Buy a piece of life for me,
Amidst this mortal host;
Permit me freedom of its use
That I may get the most.

Buy a piece of life for me
To build a just reward
Through wise and careful stewardship
That I might show my Lord.

Buy a piece of life for me
To use my talents best,
In the time allotted me
To prove I met the test.

Yes, buy a piece of life for me,
And the Master's sure to say:
"Well done my good and faithful son,
I'm glad you learned to pray."

The *Vashon*

Across the Sound the ferry goes
Carrying trucks and island cars,
When it rains, or when it sometimes snows;
Under winter skies and myriad stars,
Once over—once back: Its daily run.
The old wooden *Vashon*, chugging, plows along
Until the day and trips are done.

Goodbye Old Girl!

Upon the deck I see the deck-hands stand,
As the *Vashon* slowly pulls away from land.
Today she's gone and sails this way no more;
Now bigger ships toss waves upon the shore.
And no more gently rocking at the ferry slip,
Goodbye old girl. We'll miss your daily trip.

The Carpenter

Dad's father was a carpenter
Who sawed so straight and true
    That those who saw his work
    Cried out:
"He knows just what to do!"
Once he made a garden gate
    And even kitchen doors.
    He also made with greatest ease,
The nicest pine wood floors.
Now, dad was just the opposite,
    And nails his hammer ate.
    He made a rabbit hutch one time
That wouldn't stand up straight.
But never once he'd undertake
    to make a chair or floor—
    Although (it's true) he tried,
One time to build a woodshed door.
I'm proud to say as some may note,
    My skills are very rare,
    Somewhat like my grandpa's were,
For I can make a chair.
Don't ask me though,
    I beg and plead, in fact, I do implore,
    For I could never build a shed,
Or,
    fix a
            sagging door!

To Sue

I lost the sun unto the rain
Lost behind a cloud so big,
Our light was nearly gone.
Victorious, it shone again,
Erasing tears the cloud-burst shed.
"Yesterday," I thought, "was just,
Our days are not in vain."
Until the frightened clouds have fled
Surely as the sun must rise;
Until the moon can once more shine,
Earth will turn, as ever, with the sands of time.

A Time to Judge

It's time to take a look at life,
The path I've traveled on.
It's time for me to cogitate,
Before my time has gone.

It's time for me to judge,
As time is flying by:
Have I done the things I should,
Am I prepared to die?

If I have lived my life quite well,
Then I can wear a smile,
But if I've not done well at all
I'd better run the final mile.

Adrift in Life

      In life I float
In an open boat,
          Looking for the shore;
I climb the mast
         Of a tarnished past,
Wanting so much more.
         With a worn out sail
And a bailing pail,
         I try to stay afloat
While the canvas flaps
         And the ocean laps
Against my little boat.
         I hoarsely cry,
As the gulls soar by,
         And I lean against the taff;
But the echo voice
         Is not my choice,
Nor is the Harpie's laugh.
         Yet on I go,
With sharks below,
         And the sun hot overhead.
With a frantic prayer,
         That splits the air,
In fear I'll soon be dead.
         But I sail on
And the day is gone:
         The sun dies in the west.
Still, I cling to the mast
         And my fearful past,
While my heart beats in my chest.
         For my boat will sink,
Or so I think,
         When I cease to struggle and fight.
But I shall win,
         No matter how thin
The sail, or my waning sight.

Momma's Pie

Momma, Momma baked a pie,
Cut it up for folks to buy;
Apple with a golden top,
I'd eat so much I'd nearly pop!
Flaky crust and luscious fruit
With thick cow's cream on top to boot!
Momma, Momma I could cry,
I miss your luscious apple pie.
I hope in heaven I will see
You baking up a bunch for me.

Play the Game

The "game" is one of great import;
    Not like any other sport;
You really have to play the rules
    And cheating is done by only fools.
The game is played in every nation;
    It may be short or great duration;
The rules apply to every one:
    The winner's picked by the way they run.
Every one is fairly judged,
    Even if they slightly "fudged."
A penalty may be assessed,
    The "Referee" is not out-guessed.
End the game in honesty
    For rewards you'll earn eternally.
What you want is what you'll get
    If goals are high which you have set.
Speed is not what you will need,
    But morals high and kindly deed.

I Saw Them Mourn

I saw them mourn, in black, my passing;
Sadly lined beside the open grave,
On the sloping hillside, green with grass,
Rich with budding flowers.

The sky, of purest blue, nestled fluffy clouds;
Clouds that pressed down against the earth;
The brown earth, fresh dug, lies a heap,
Waiting to be thrown upon the dead.
Cover up the lifeless clay with dirt,
Buried; all to soon forgotten by the world.
Tear stained faces, unashamed,
Lined in sorrow for the now departed,

Who, standing, watching: liberated;
Far more free than those that mourn.
I saw the beauty of the church,
Old and white, surrounded by my kind.

The stones that mark the resting place
Of those who've gone before,
With moss and fungi spots of age,
Suggest the tenure of the body here interred.

Would that I could help them in the wake;
To ease the pain they feel.
But wait they must, until their day,
When they will stand unseen;

Having crossed the veil from life
Into the paradise of God,
Where they will watch the sad array
Pay tribute to a family or, the passing of a friend.

"T" Time

        A model "T",
Or so it's said,
        Is loud enough to wake the dead.
It shakes and rattles and coughs and sputs
        And bounces in the muddy ruts.
But every boy I've ever known
        Would like to have one of his own.

San Juan Park

Sunday fun, for kids like me,
Were picnics at the beach and park,
Looking at a glassy sea
Beneath a pleasant summer sun.
Softball in a short grassed field;
Old ball bats and tattered gloves.
Shouts and hoots of happy kids
Climbing in a maple tree,
With kelp beds rising on the tide.
Looking at a glassy sea.

A Trip to the Mainland

Wind blown fir trees,
Needles shed;
Rain clouds threatening overhead.
        Freeway traffic flying by,
        Cars and trucks assault the eye,
        Wildly changing lane to lane;
Headlights from a passing train.
Scenery passes in review,
Trucks with trailers, not a few;
        Smoke from tail pipes choke my lungs;
        Roadside ladder with broken rungs.
        Cumulus nimbi, storm cells dead,
Threaten sunshine overhead,
As welcome respite from the rain.
I hope the sunshine comes again.

Taste-bud Temptation

From the islands where I grew,
Feast on salmon do;
Or make a brew
Of oyster stew
That's fit for me and you.

Times Have Changed

I've never thought my dad was mean,
    Though strict he was it's true.
I never thought my mom was cruel
    When forced to carry in the fuel:
Fire wood against the winter's cold
    (That's what we used in days of old).

Because they made mistakes in life:
    Not an always perfect wife—
Nor dad a perfect dad for us;
    (A couple times I heard him cuss!)
We didn't judge them then or now,
    They were parents learning how . . .

To raise their kids the best they could.
    So, we carried in the wood;
Cut the kindling and the grass;
    Went to school each grade to pass.
Times have changed an awful lot,
    Such magic things the kids have got!

And laws upon the lawyer's books
    Defining how a family looks;
How to raise your child just-so
    And if you don't, to jail you'll go.
Blame your parents for your faults,
    Lock them up in iron vaults!

Parents failed to raise you right?
    Blame them for your sorry plight.
Yes, times have changed as we can see;
    If something's wrong . . . well,
        Just blame me.

I Let My Honored Dead Depart

Today I saw upon my head
Ten generations of the dead.
Each one had his children there;
Each one seemed as though to stare
And all were reaching out to me
With records in their hands to see.
I turned my back and went my way
(As if my actions seemed to say:
"Be gone, I haven't time for you;
I have other things to do!").

Today I walked another way
And watched my earthly frame decay.
Standing in the judgment dock
I saw ten generations walk;
Each one passed and shook his head;
All were of my lineage dead.
Not one came to welcome me,
The Judge declared: "Thus it shall be!"
The justice hall stood grim and bare,
My footsteps only echoed there.
The message tattooed on my heart:
I let my honored dead depart.

INDEX

A Modest Hero, 36
A Time to Judge, 69
A Timely Thought, 23
A Trip to the Mainland, 74
About Love, 56
Adrift in Life, 70
Another Wild Rose, 57
Answer to "The Daisies", 25
Blast Those Wild Roses!, 47
Buy a Piece of Life, 66
Cattle Point, 46
Deep Snow, 64
Determination, 26
Do You Ever Think of Me?, 11
Dusting, 8
Feeling Nature, 16
Fly My Flag, 31
Fly or Float, 39
Food Stuff, 38
Friday's Bay, 15
Goodbye Old Girl, 67
Has Summer Passed?, 47
I Let My Honored Dead Depart, 76
I Love a Cow, 52
I Placed the Wreath, 30
I Saw Them Mourn, 72
I'd Pick More Daisies, 24
In Retrospect, 17
Islands in the Sound, 8
Islands Rising From the Sea, 10
It's Late, 22
Just a Thought, 44
Knowledge, 26
Little Yellow Gold Finch, 58
Memories, 2
Momma's Pie, 71
Oh, Precious Little Imp, 55

Orcas Belle, 39
Perfection, 26
Pictures, 41
Play the Game, 71
Portland Fair, 12
Remember Me?, 28
Rosa Mendoza, 40
San Juan Park, 73
Sarah Ruth of Straight Answers, 14
Snow Flakes, 64
Soft Shoulders, 13
"T" Time, 73
Taste-bud Temptation, 74
The Book Report, 44
The Carpenter, 68
The Circus Came to Town, 12
The Good Old Days, 3
The Rain, 56
The Separator, 20
The Smells I Like, 35
The Snowman, 64
The Song of Love, 51
The Sound, 49
The Valley Church, 18
The *Vashon*, 67
They Came Here Just Ahead of Me, 4
Thought for Tonight, 22
Times Have Changed, 75
To a Queen, 48
To Gomez, 34
To Mom, 50
To Sue, 69
When I Was Five, 6
Where Lady Slippers Grow, 2
Wild Pink Roses, 54
Winter at the Door, 63
Winter Winds, 60